My Glamorous Assistant

To Jennie + Roy

and a Peaceful New Year

Cath Nichols

My Glamorous Assistant

Cath Nichols

HEADLAND

First published in 2007
by
HEADLAND PUBLICATIONS
38 York Avenue
West Kirby, Wirral
CH48 3JF

British Library cataloguing in Publication Data.
A full CIP record for this book is available from the British Library
ISBN
1 902096 40 7

Printed in Great Britain by
L. Cocker Ltd.
Unit A9, Prospect Street, Liverpool L6 1AU

HEADLAND acknowledges the financial support
of Arts Council England

ARTS COUNCIL ENGLAND

Acknowledgements

Some of the poems previously appeared in the following: *Citizen 32*, *In the Red*, *Iota*, *Orbis*, *Rain Dog*, *Smiths Knoll*, *Smoke*, *The Rialto*. The sequences 'Dust series' and 'Warning' were first published in *Red Ink*. Several of the poems from 'High Wire (Woolworths Suite)' were in *Watermark* (FLAX Books, 2007). 'Bambi Woods' appeared in the anthology *The Dead Good Poets Society: The Book* (Headland, 2005). 'The Tallest Building in the World' won first prize in the Originals Poetry Competition 2006. 'Corona' was recorded for the OXFAM 'Life Lines' Poetry CD (2006), and 'Parmesan' was recorded for the RNIB version of 'Life Lines'.

Thanks to Michael Cunningham, Sarah Hymas, Aileen La Tourette and Clare Potter for editorial suggestions. Finally, thanks to the Arts Council of England north-west for enabling the Woolworths Suite to be toured in Liverpool, Cardiff and New York.

CONTENTS

VANISHING ACT

Snow White 10
Never 11
Bambi Woods 12
Away from here: Nevada Desert 14
Too Much 15
Sideways 16
Thundernails 21
Dust series 22
A tea party 24

THE RING

The weakest point 28
Winter light 29
Tombstone Cowboy 30
Second Chance 31
Threshold 33
Second Sight 34
Grace 35
Blue 36

HIGH WIRE (WOOLWORTHS SUITE)

Fear of Falling 38
The tallest building in the world (1913) 39
How to be Beautiful 40
Worship 41
The magician's assistant 42
A 1930s Deal 43
Doris Day's apron gives an interview 44
Setting 45
Stone 46

CONTENTS *(Continued)*

My name 47
Here I am 48
'Where sixpence works wonders' 49
At the haberdashery counter 50
Treading water 51
Treading water II 52
The beautiful words that I had are gone 53
Volts 54
Music in the wires 55

KNIFE THROWER

Warning 1 58
In black and white 60
Warning 2 61
Reckless Sleeper 62
Warning 3 63
Iain Stansfield would have been good for me 64
Parmesan 65
Electra Complex 67
Silent Type 68
Written in Ice 69
The further adventures of Electra 70
Shift 72
Corona 73
Rapunzel 74

Notes 75

For

Pip
my X and ace photographer.

Martin (always glamorous and ever helpful)
for the book cover design and my website
www.cathnichols.com

VANISHING ACT

Snow White

I won't write about my childhood as other people do,
instead I shall write about apples, shiny red apples,
like the ones plucked by ladies in disguise –
virgins' Step-mothers, wicked Queens.
More and more I see things from their point of view,
lay hands upon the Gala, Braeburn and Red Russet,
grab green/red ones too, the Coxes and Pink Ladies –
the apples with two sides.

I used to wolf down Granny Smiths till the dentist said
acid had eroded my enamel; showed me the x-rays.
Afterwards I looked for safer diet options,
took to eating red apples. Bland, red apples.
(This was as an adult, please note, not as a child.
I don't remember eating apples as a child).

Never

Never park on double yellows,
pay your library fines on time,
never steal a friend's lover,
never make the promise *never*.
Never have her name tattooed
on your back or bicep.
Never cut your hair like hers
just because *she* likes it.
Never do that thing
with half a heart each,
two silver chains,
together we are one.
Never break a heart for fun
to prove you're on the mend.
Never sleep with someone
to gain the upper hand.

Never go to Home Sweet Home,
grow roses round your heart.
Never lift the latch to girls
who might be carol-singing wolves.
But if you do slip up this way
and sense her closing in – soft
and sweet as ice-cream melt, warm
and quiet as wings – resist,
and arm yourself:
keep bleach beneath the sink
to scrub out the lip-prints,
the footprints,
she'll leave upon your skin,
the never-ever-always-be-here
the never-ever-love-forever
the never-ever-sorry-baby
the never-ever, *ever* –

Bambi Woods

The producer of Debbie Does Dallas
named his star Bambi Woods: *Bambi,*
after the little deer, and woods
for a deer in the woods.
It wasn't deep, he laughs.

It makes me think. Could she've
been instead, Bunny Meadows?
Or the exotic dancer: Gerbila Burrows
– dark eyes, lithe limbs –
always typecast as the desert princess,
though she was born in Bromley.
I smell stale sweat, and over the wall
next door's kids are cleaning out
the *femme fatale's* nemesis,
the good-girl perma-virgin Miss Mousie Hole.
Another year and she'll progress
to more challenging roles:
the demure slut of suburbia
outwardly treading the straight and narrow,
in private always up for a party. Wild,
but only in front of her husband,
or the occasional camera crew.

Down the yard my guinea pig, Ms Piggy Hutch,
struts glossy hindquarters like an NYPD cop
and cracks blue jokes
in a South American accent.
She is the muscular one, the heavyweight dyke,
who keeps them all in line. She gets to play
the brothel madam, the scary dom,
the one in uniform ... Beneath this tough,
gleaming exterior her curves are still hoping
for something.You see, unlike in the scripts ...
but I'm getting carried away and the sun has gone in.

I go inside and reflect: Bambi Woods vanished
after her film was made. My pet porn stars
go back to eating sunflower seeds and grass.
Occasionally get up to tread mills.

Away from here

1. Nevada Desert

There's a man comes in who only does kissing
makes out it's for real, wants a girl to fall for him.
You'd think it would be easy to fake that deal
but it's a hard trick to pull – and he takes the full hour.

I know we're paid to compliment their dicks,
praise their style, humour their favourite kinks,
but his game is dangerous; you have to stay so sharp,
afterwards he asks, *Was it business or pleasure, honey?*

and I reply *Sweetheart, with you it's always fun,*
and I take his money.

His rescue fantasy's sick – a john's bent power trip.
He's not Richard Gere, and I ain't no pretty woman.

I bought a fast car, with my own money,
stuffed the back seat with cuddly toys.

I can always get away from here.

2. Too Much

I come here because the women are hot.
Women on the streets are too much trouble –
crackheads, diseased. Here they stay clean,
or they're out. I come here because the women

are hot. Women on the streets are too much
trouble, they're looking to rip me off.
Some look at me with those dead-fish eyes;
but no-one makes them take those drugs,

or drink. Women on the streets want more
than I can give: dinner, a house, kids. To talk.
Endless talk, it drives you mad!
I come here because the women are hot,

and women on the streets are too much trouble.
Money's all that's on their minds, they're always
wanting more. They talk too much,
women on the streets – not like here.

Sideways

Does my fanny look big in this?
She stands, legs apart, pointing to the soft-edged V,
makes eye-contact with me; I dead-pan back.

She *does* mean front fanny, fanny/ lips
and not the American, fanny/ bum.
She turns
front then side then front
smoothing her thighs.

We're getting ready to go out, and maybe
she's thinking: Will they be looking?
The way straight women look at men.

She means: are my trousers too tight?
She means: I am a straight woman going
to my first all-women party and maybe
I don't know how to behave. Maybe
I don't know what will happen.

For the record, Becca is energetic,
pretty, has curly black hair, and she talks a lot.
On the side, Becca is a pole-dancer.
We see a demonstration later at the party
without the pole.

Far from flocking
to this foxy full-on madam
the dance creates a lesbian Red Sea
/
disruption
not least because her limbs don't fit the music
don't fit the ambience, instead demand ATTENTION!

I fade onto a sofa, keep watch.
A woman sits down, leans in
and whispers – incredulous – into my hair
Do you know *her?*

*

In the theatre Becca dances
'Homeostasis: Fight or Flight',
I think this means a search for balance.
Two dancers move at speed, narrowly avoid
collision. They duck and flinch and spasm,
moving to a soundtrack of instruction
that issues from a soothing female voice:
'Anxiety ... people who take on too much responsibility –
which leads us to deep breathing and breath control.
Don't worry if you find this difficult.'
The dancers find it hard to keep their balance.

*

It's late, the stars are out and high.
My friend and I get Becca outside, into the cul-de-sac.
She resists (she hasn't pulled; I'm sure she's peeved).
Bonfire smoke trails over us, we breathe it in, relax.

Becca talks

about a woman at the lap-dancing club,
an 'old hand' who, in the course of her audition
asks to see her fanny, feels her up
Some kind of sex   or not-sex /sex
takes place

(something internal)

Becca tells this story sideways
without emotion.
Yet it's shaped like a street fight without
the muscles, with less clothes and less dirt
than gunslingers
in a stand-off
at the OK Angel Corral:
a show of bravado

glitter
straight between the eyes

She is nineteen or twenty-two …
and likes to know what you think –
how else will she know what to feel?
She is trying so hard and trying hard to look
unstudied.
What keeps us from falling/ failing?

How do you make the sound of speech
without moving your lips?
Each dancer struggles to articulate herself.
Eventually we all find a way to fake it,
to pass as normal, to pass as human,
learn the art of ventriloquism.

On stage Becca dances. Her breath rasps out
stacatto. Gestures ricochet between the dancers.
Speed might break them, but it doesn't.
Is this what saves us? This
constant, moving surface,
the dazzle and glare we project?

The voice recording is on a loop. It comes
from Speilburger's book, 'Understanding Stress and Anxiety'
and Houlden's classic, 'Ventriloquism for Beginners':

'Anxiety ... people who take on too much responsibility –
which leads us to deep breathing and breath control.
Don't worry if you find this difficult.'

Becca talks
of boys in clubs and bars
those her own age
she keeps
inside her phone
they often call or text
some   are anxious for her
some   are drama for her
She is always in demand, always
getting caught
She has so much front I bet she
rubbishes
their heroic attempts to look out for her

*

On stage there is a box one foot
square, painfully hard to ascend.
Once there her tics lessen. It is a
perch from which to try a new
vocabulary of movement. There's
a picture on the side from
Houlden's guide: a cross-section
of the mouth and nose with arrows
projecting the sounds 'M' > and 'N' >

'....you have to push your tongue right back into your mouth
to throttle back the air... this will give a muffled sound.'

> *M-a*
> *N-a*

A second dancer insinuates herself
onto the box; grapples with Becca.

Both try to stand upright. Trying
to communicate is dangerous –

physically, we might over-balance,
verbally, the tongue hangs heavy in the mouth.

Does my fanny look big in this?

She likes to know you are watching –
how else will she know she is here?

'you have to push your tongue right back
to throttle back the air… this will give a muffled sound.'

Becca talks a lot.
Then dances.

Thundernails

No-one knows that underneath the desert path,
the road track she stood on, underneath
the thundernails, underneath the sound
there was the sea. And she crouched down
covered her ears and thought of the lady
in the pink and white dress, the black lady
on the bicycle, dress flared out.
And she thought of the blond man's back,
she thought of the blond square dog,
the music they made, the guitar. And
the thundernails kept /* /* /* And she thought
'beneath the underneath there is the sea.'

Dust series

1. There was a swift response to the missing person's report

We couldn't clean it up   till the red and white
tape   came down
black smears
round door frames
not white   like you'd think
dusting for prints

(This was before
cop dramas   showed us everything)

A woman comes to collect my prints, rolling
each tip across the form, *For elimination,*
she says. This surprises me – the rolling,
I'd thought they'd press my fingers down flat
like finger-painting in school only in black.

2. news

we ate chicken burgers with green chillies
waiting for the police
(and me a vegetarian)

we talked about her
chocolate
marzipan

in Thornton's
a sales assistant
tells someone

                                        I don't know
                              who doesn't know me
                    who doesn't know Jeanette

didn't know   Jeanette

there's a body in a lake
she heard it
on the radio.

I walk out
invisible

run
for the bus

3. fault/ line

her mother	whom she never spoke to
holds us responsible	says
not to go	to the funeral.
So	
we plant roses	
but no amount of poetry	can save us

A tea party

My mother's mouth shaped 'O', and her eyes blinked fast.

I felt her pull the back of my shirt,
and her mouth shaped 'O', and her eyes blinked fast.

We stumbled down the laddered stairs, my mother, sister, friend and me.
I felt her pull the back of my shirt,
and her mouth was shaping 'O' and her eyes were blinking fast.

I looked at my sister, Isle, who frowned, and did not speak.
We stumbled down the laddered stairs, my mother, sister, friend and me.
I felt her pull the back of my shirt,
and her mouth was shaping 'O' and her eyes were blinking fast.

We'd been to tea with Hedwig Potthast, and she'd wanted to show us
Heinrich's 'little room'.
I looked at my sister, Isle, who frowned, and did not speak.
We stumbled down the laddered stairs, my mother, sister, friend and me.
I felt her pull the back of my shirt,
and her mouth was shaping 'O' and her eyes were blinking fast.

Before the door was shut I saw a chair made out of bones.
We'd been to tea at Hedwig Potthast's, and she'd wanted to show us
Heinrich's 'little room'.
I looked at my sister, Isle, who frowned, and did not speak.
We stumbled down the laddered stairs, my mother, sister, friend and me.
I felt a pull on the back of my shirt,
and her mouth was shaping 'O' and her eyes were blinking fast.

A lamp spun veins of red into that attic room.
Before the door was shut I saw a chair made out of bones.
We'd been to tea at Hedwig's, and she'd wanted to show us
Heinrich's 'little room'.

I looked at my sister, Isle, who frowned, and did not speak.
We stumbled down the laddered stairs, my mother, sister, friend and me.
I felt mama pull the back of my shirt, and
her mouth was shaping 'O' and her eyes were blinking fast.

There was a lampshade made the same in my living room ...
In the attic, before the door was shut I saw a chair made of bones.
We'd been to tea at Hedwig's, and she'd wanted to show us
Heinrich's 'little room'.
I looked at my sister, Isle, who frowned, and did not speak.
We stumbled down the laddered stairs, my mother, sister, friend and me.
Mama pulled me back by my shirt –
her mouth was shaping 'O' and her eyes were blinking fast.

At home my mother grabbed the lamp and threw it out: a gift
from Himmler, in our living room, the lampshade bright like skin.
In the attic there had been a chair made out of bones;
we'd been to tea at Hedwig Potthast's, and she'd wanted to show us
Heinrich's 'little room'.
I looked at my sister, Isle, who frowned, and did not speak.
We stumbled down the laddered stairs, my mother, sister, friend and me.
I feel her pulling the back of my shirt, see
her mouth shaping 'O' and her eyes blinking fast.

My mother cried, and would not speak of why.
At home she'd grabbed the lamp and thrown it out, a gift
from Himmler, in our living room, the lampshade bright like skin.
In the attic there had been a chair made out of bones;
we'd been to tea at Hedwig Potthast's, and she'd wanted to show us
Heinrich's 'little room'.
I looked at my sister, Isle, who frowned, and did not speak.
We stumbled down the laddered stairs, my mother, sister, friend and me.
Mama pulled me back by my shirt –
her mouth was shaping 'O' and her eyes were blinking fast.

THE RING

The weakest point

I didn't know how we would support the dome
until we were close to raising it.
I was a draughtsman, not yet an architect.
We puzzled on my fancy turret resting
on the dome's weakest point,
devised an inner frame, a cone
peaking beneath its base.
The dome itself then billowed outward
like a piecrust skirt.
The *piece de resistance* a false ceiling,
in proportion to the nave below.
Circles upon circles.

Finally the job is done. Nothing can be added
to the beauty of light.
Some say it is a travesty, 'the congregant looks up
and thinks, not of God, but of Wren!'
This is the voice of jealousy. For I am
the only man who's seen it through: planned
a cathedral and lived to see it built.
But I'm out-of-favour now. I'm
ninety-one and I've outlived
so many friends and family.
I should have been a physician,
concentrated on the small things:

the louse,
the eye of a fly;

the woman
I delayed in marrying;

my son.

Winter light

the woman at the window
throws back a curtain   looses

light and its diagonals   she draws
her towelling gown closer to   her ears

appear through loose strands
of hair   she turns to you

and brings the pale morning light
in her hands   across the floor

a gift   she folds her felted body
back into the duvet   presses

a cold ear to your collar bone
a cold hand to your chest

Tombstone Cowboy

On waking he felt his hips were lighter,
on pushing back the sheet he recognised the morgue,
on looking for his clothes he found another's,
walked lop-sided through the doors.

Without a sling or gun he felt much smaller,
moved from house to house with nervous stealth,
saw a shop with feather boas in the window,
plus some holsters and a Stetson – all for sale.

He broke the glass and took them, leapt about
against the siren, jumped a wall and hit
the playground, ran the field, then slowed his pace.
Slung the belt on, evened out his stride.

Second Chance

We feared the knife, not the death
from hanging. We knew they took
the bodies down and cut them up
for science. It wasn't allowed
but they had to learn somehow,
and our souls weren't worth protecting.

But we feared this butchery:
without a proper body, proper burial,
how can a man be resurrected?
Oxford Gaol – godforsaken hole –
they rolled cut bodies down the dry moat,
left them to rot with kitchen waste.

No-one would go there to take the dead away
Jenks' curse held them back, so bodies lay
unclaimed – and the knife marks lay hidden.
I knew I'd sprawl in death there, without
even the dignity of folded arms for prayer,
not even right side up to beg for my soul's

mercy. If lucky, I might have a handkerchief
of cabbage leaf fall over my lolling head.

*

Even with friends dragging on my legs
to speed things up, I took all of thirty minutes
to die. Then they carted my body off, and
it gave them the shock of their lives:
their knife stuck in – I gave a cry!
Scared them good and proper, I did.

Doctors called the judges. Judges
called a meeting, called for new witnesses.
Good news for me then – they were scared
to repeat the execution. If I had died
and risen again, God mustn't want me dead.
You can see it from their point of view:

it might be unwise to fly in the face
of a miracle... they found a midwife.
She was found to say
her child was still-born,
so I couldn't be a child murderer,
could I?

*

I moved away. Being a miracle was hard
on my nerves. I had a chance to marry, so
I grabbed it. Of course we had children. And
even though my husband thought it strange,
I kept hold
of the shroud.

Threshold

From a distance I see it as if through
a fish-tank: a sudden shower of pollen,
dust-powder rain.

Thick sparkles, a foreground for dark rhododendron.
Summer's snow-shaker,
slow-motion glitter.

Curtains of the stuff falling.
Slow golden vision.

Second Sight

I was fifteen when I birthed her in a cave
near the Dropping Well. People are scared of there –
that stream can turn a fallen stick to stone. I knew
I'd be left alone, though I took someone with me.
She wasn't much use, complaining of the heat, minding
the thunder – said they were portents. Then she said
she could smell *sulphur* when the baby came!
That's *all* I needed to keep the rumours going. My baby:
born out-of-wedlock, deformed, and now from hell.

They took me to court for selling myself (*incontinency*
they called it. I call it getting paid for my trouble).
I gave the judge what for: *two* of his servants were
with child – with child to him. He shut up then…
I got baby Ursula baptised. You are surprised – 'child
of the devil' and all? Well, that's my secret. I knew
a few things beyond the Judge's roving eye (and other parts),
some information on the Bishop. They say my child
has a different kind of eye. Like me, she knows things.

I gave her up to a foster mother. I couldn't
fight her corner when the 'witch' insults flew.
Ursula is married now, and has the ear of gentlefolk.
No children yet … Folk are afraid as before, but this time
with her Cave and crooked back, her stick, her rhymes
and prophesies, there is respect (she plays the game well).
And of course, for her there is also a husband.
She stands the right side of that line
does my daughter 'Mother' Shipton.

Grace

Mount Grace Priory near Osmotherly

The Pope declares our order pure,
'Cartusia numquam reformata,
quia numquam deformata.'
We need no reformation, for
we have never bent our Rule.
At this Charterhouse we have (on loan,
we do not own as individuals) three rooms:
a bedroom, study and shrine.
To some this would be paradise,
a house of one's own, eternal peace.
'Stat crux dum volvitur orbis.'
The Cross is steady while the world turns.

This world is small. We are alone
with God always.
The outside world may only enter
through the hands of our lay brothers.
One has brought me thyme for the garden.
We do not speak.
I love the tiny, hidden flowers,
the smell of wet earth.

Blue

A blue roan horse is beautiful
in mist beneath the tree.
The hedge-thorns flag wet skeins of wool
(a blue roan horse is beautiful).
Dawn follows night; there is a lull
and dark eyes suspend me.
A blue roan horse is beautiful
in mist beneath the tree.

HIGH WIRE
(WOOLWORTHS SUITE)

Fear of Falling

A fresh egg was placed

gently

in the lift carriage.
Cables were cut
and the lift
fell
fifty-five
floors.

Journalists and
potential tenants
gathered
at ground level,
waiting.

The lift arrived.
As Frank had stated:
their safety mechanisms
were second to none.

The egg was unbroken.

The Tallest Building in the World (1913)

Not a hard interview, no, I was chosen
because I'm five foot four,
shorter than him that owns this place.
We're all blonde too,
and wear white gloves, a smart uniform.
Mr Woolworth likes to see me
close the doors, press the buttons.
I like to sew at home;
I have small hands and a neat way
with my fingers (I come
from a family of weavers). The lifts,
they say, have triple safety features,
and stop to within an eighteenth
of an inch on every floor.
I'm the spider plumbing depths
between a girdered web. Here,
there's such precision. I think of
a shuttle, zooming back and forth,
crossing the weft of each floor,
filling in the picture of an empire
built on dimes and cents. It's a
fairy-tale palace for the 20th century,
with electric lights on every floor!
They say it's like the parliament in England.
They call it the new gothic.
This is a *sky scraper.* My Dad says
that's what they used to call
a ship's tallest mast. So, in my lift
I am a sailor in the rigging,
criss-crossing ... up and down.

How to be Beautiful

First assess your raw material: much can be done with very little.
Remember, red lipstick is an instant fix, but a 'natural' look
takes patience. A good haircut goes without saying,
as does decent underwear – dress from the inside out.
The art of beauty is in the finish, not the substance,
as Jayne Mansfield once said: *You're only as good as your base.*
So don't forget to moisturise; apply your foundation with due
consideration. Next work on your eyes: pluck, shadow, blend.
Then blend some more. Apply blusher sparingly, and
fill in your lips.

Effects such as pink or yellow on eyelids, silver or black
on lips, only look good on models and teenagers.
Have people think you're young for your age, rather than
a raddled forty-something. The eye of the beholder
can be fooled: a well cut dress can distract from flaws,
and a well-chosen compliment: *My that colour suits you!*
will help others see *you* in a more flattering light.
Be a good listener. You will be expected to glow
from within, and since one cannot be pregnant all the time,
a shiny, scrubbed down soul is the next best thing.

Do not forget your true hair colour. Be kind
to animals, but buy the best make-up you can afford.
Be lady-like. Never let your husband see you
cutting your toenails. Remember: frown lines are forever.
Invest in a quality concealer.
Aim to be yourself. Try not to be seen
to be trying; make the effort look effortless; smile.
And *never* let the sun go down on your anger.

Worship

It's on Church Street: a brass cross,
flattened into the pavement, small;
marks where the old church was.
They pulled it down, put up a shop instead.
The Catholics were calmed with talk
of a new cathedral up on Hope Street.

It was the first Woolworth's store.
And when I say first, I mean *really* first.
First in the country, not just on Merseyside.
We were that proud.
First day Woolworth's opened its doors
no sales were made, it was for 'viewing only'

and a free pot of tea in the tea rooms.
There was a brass band too – we had a ball.
But the Daily Mail was cruel: said that Woolworth
was a chancer like Barnum – a circus-man!
Said he'd only chosen Liverpool, so when
it all went belly-up, he could scarper back

to America; the docks being so handy, like. Pffh!
The next day, its first proper day,
there were queues outside,
and most of the counters bare by evening.
We proved them all wrong:
we can shop as good as anyone.

The magician's assistant

Whilst we wait for
                                        The Man
            let me tell you about
                        my lipsticked mouth (my teeth)
                                    my beautiful ring (my nails)
                                                my sparkling shoes (my toes)...

                        I want to go home.
I want to click my heels together
                                                    and go home.

I have red shoes with sequins,
and though I'm not from Kansas
I don't think that matters. It's about
                                        how much you want it.
But I can't click my heels –
my left foot is poking out of this hole and I can't
move my right foot towards it without
losing my balance, and that would be dangerous
because this cabinet is only just
            wide enough
                                  and tall enough
                                                and deep enough
to hold me. If I bring my feet together I will fall.

And besides I have no time:
the audience is waiting.

A 1930s deal

It's only the men that are married here.
Us shop girls are single women, we'll leave
when we find the right man. Mind, we have
a good time whilst kicking our heels to be wed.
We sell children's clothes, paper patterns,
haberdashery. We make our clothes at home, see,

except maybe for lingerie … and socks.
They let us have discounted stock, so
we'll make up the clothes then tell
the customers how easy it is, and
what a fair deal they're getting: *this skirt, see,*
it practically made itself!

But we don't have hunting knives.
Can you imagine? My supervisor says
they stocked them when the store first opened.
Frank Woolworth thought they'd be popular –
they'd sold so well in Canada! Honest!
And we've got tin toys, sheet music,

Christmas decorations… all sorts,
and everything for under sixpence.
We work five and one half days.
The store pays us for our breaks
and part pays our hot meals.
There's not many'd do that for you.

It's a very good deal.

Doris Day's apron gives an interview

I am stupid because I cook home-made soup and pasta;
        I bake biscuits, crumbles and cakes.
You are clever because you only make roast dinners,
        cooked breakfasts, or order in take-aways.

I am stupid because I tell you about my dreams,
        and I talk through TV movies.
You are clever because in silence
        you hold on to the remote.

I lose my temper and get upset,
        but you are a Vulcan.
I need you like shoes need laces,
        and you wear slip-ons.

I am stupid. I have forgotten
        something important.
You are clever, and too much
        of a gentleman to mention it.

Setting

Whilst we wait for
The Man
let me tell you about
my lipsticked mouth (my teeth)
my beautiful ring (my nails)
my sparkling shoes (my toes)...

There's a space here for my hand
enough to wave,
to stroke,
to implore,
to display my nails,
my jewellery.
Don't they look pretty?

Sometimes I feel my hands aren't part of me,
they hold and lift and carry, slice
and cut and clean and chop, and
feed and clear away. I keep my nails
short because there's so much to do.
But when I put my hands outside the box
I wear false nails.

See how long and fancy they are?
How Languorous. How Beautiful.
I waft across the stage
shimmery and translucent,
appearing and disappearing,
graceful, elegant, ornamental.
Not suitable for everyday use.

Stone

There is a stone
in her hand
that feels like lead
there is lead
upon her heart
that feels like truth
there is a truth
beneath her brow
that feels like flint
feels like an axe
feels like splitting.

My name

I'm Meirion Evans, I'm twenty-seven.
I'm Meirion Evans, I'm twenty-seven.
I keep on saying it, over and over.
I'm Meirion Evans.
I'm Meirion Evans.

I talk to people in the night.
They bring me medicine
then I sleep without dreams.
But when awake   sometimes –

I feel a loud noise ripping through the ship. I see
a boy with dark hair letting go of his toy train.
It skids down the deck. We list: above us the lifeboats
sway inboard on their chains. In panic men cut them
free but they land on deck! Heavy, unstoppable
they grind a path after the train, crush passengers,
leave limbs in their wake,
bodies against the railings.

Not me.
I am falling
                    slowly   into water.
          Or I am still
                              and the sky falls   against me.

They bring me medicine and then
I sleep without dreams.
But when awake   sometimes –

Someone tells me it took
just eighteen minutes.
Eighteen minutes! and such a liner,
such a beauty, the Lusitania is sunk.

Silence, then a ripping in my head.

Here I am

a mouth
a hand
some toes
about to disappear.

I am dismembered, but
my slices stay stacked
held upright by this box.

The wounds heal. But
I get scared when I lie down.

I was in bed this afternoon, with the curtains drawn.
I thought: if I lie still, the mattress might catch
the loosened parts as they fall away from me;
the blanket might stop them as they roll away from me;
slide off the bed, and run away from me.

I thought: if I shut my eyes
I might not be here anymore.

‘Where sixpence works wonders’

The VP Twin camera is sold in three parts:
the camera body, backplate and a choice
of camera case. Each part costing sixpence.
We build an empire, you build a camera.

A way to buy exactly what you need,
bit by bit. Ideal for today’s careful housewife
or pocket-moneyed child. *Nothing*
more than sixpence, a pricing guarantee.
Tin soldiers, tiny tubes of Snowfire lipstick,
two razor blades, instead of packs of five.
We build an empire, you build a camera.

Saucepans sold without their lids
(or buy the lid for sixpence too),
and socks and shoes come singly
(for the thrifty, one-legged man).
Nothing more than sixpence, a pricing guarantee.
But when playing cards are taxed at thruppence
our margins are squeezed. We think you think:

It’s good to know where my money is going,
so we keep our pricing guarantee
by charging for the tax separately.
Lighters, too, are more expensive:
so sixpence to the store, sixpence to
the Treasury. We build an empire,
you build a camera. We think you think:

Every part has its value, every man his worth.
A nickel, a dime. Sixpence.
VP Twin camera, sold in three parts.

At the haberdashery counter

This is my sister's counter. I work round there
on Sweets. People think I'm lucky, but truth be told
I haven't got much of a sweet tooth. I'd swap
with Netty in a flash – but she won't hear of it.
Still at least I get to dream on my breaks.
I like the fabric here, the printed cotton, voile,

the embroidery. Sometimes they even have silk,
you'd be surprised. See, when I've had too much
of sherbet pips and glassy gobbers (that's what
I call gobstoppers) a ream of blue velvet
takes my mind off things. I come round here,
Netty doesn't mind. It's not that I hate sweets,

it's just we had this aunt when I was a child,
and she only had one eye. They didn't tell me.
I remember going into a darkened room,
and there she was in bed propped up. And
bedside her, in a glass this one eyeball
all   white   shine. She'd survived the bombing

of the Lusitania, but never got back to America.
Stayed near Dadda, her brother … I like to think
she'd like my job at Woolies; be proud.
Me Dadda said she left Wales cause she wanted
to see the Woolworth tower – tallest building
in the world in 1913. Still is.

She used to show me this picture printed on
a packet of sewing needles, one of Woolie's
best sellers back then: seventy-nine needles
for tuppence ha'penny, *'Made in England'*.
Red paper folded over – with that skyscraper
tower plumb down the middle.

Treading water

Would it be too obvious to mention
coffins? But this is upright, more
like a cask, a keg I stand up in.

In the dark, I wait,
a knuckled seahorse,
poised, nervous, precise.

Another girl has the real coffin:
the *lady sawn in half* girl.
I wonder what she thinks about?

Treading water II

I hear stars like thunder in the dark. The nurse
pushing her trolley. Sparks flare beneath my skin.
My name is Meirion Evans.
I am twenty-seven.

I went to see my sister in America,
but we are at war, and my mother called me home.
I want to go back.

They bring me medicine and then
I sleep without dreams.
But when I am awake –

My name is Merion Evans and I come from Wales.
I feel myself going down, going under. I have
a fever. I talk to people in the night. They tell me
there's bodies still being found.

I sleep without dreams, but when I am awake
there are shooting stars. Sparks. They tell me I
have lost an eye. Though I'm treading water now,
on my side, I will not get back to America.

The beautiful words that I had are gone

Let me tell you about my lipsticked mouth, my teeth.
Let me tell you about what I taste in my mouth

the words I use to cover up the taste
of people, the sight of people.

I see them, I hear them too, and they speak
and they move more beautifully than me,

they find their seats; they talk, graciously.
I would like to have more beautiful words

but the ones that I had
are gone.

My mouth shapes itself, and shapes itself
and cannot settle.

I dress with care. I paint my lips.
I show my teeth.

But all that I had is gone.
… My hands…

I smooth my frock. I press my lips together.

Volts

I once knew a girl – a woman, really,
but girl-like in her frame – who said
(eventually) that ECT was, *well.... all right.*

It didn't frighten her as much as other things.
It filled the hole in her head that otherwise
filled up with too much brightness.

I once knew a girl

she had small thin scars like bird-tracks running
across her face and arms. She hardly ate
and watched the birds run, so panicked

so terribly lost.

When things were at their worst she'd turn
her face to the ward: then blessed volts
would shock her mind from her skull.

Music in the wires

There's a rhythm in the lift, in the cogs
and wheels of it, the wires and cables,
tensions and a minor third.
There's an harmonic interval
the sound of whole numbers
whole vessels filled with water,
a note, a swell, a roar,
a resonance that seems just right.
Music fills the wires.
(Blow through a blade of grass
and you'll also find this hum.)

Sometimes in the lift I become
the white-gloved heart
of a singing, soaring comet;
and when its choir exceeds
the speed of sound I take off,
punch through the roof and fly.
Else I lift the building too;
drag Woolworth's monument
through clouds and layers of blue
– bricks crumbling from our tail
pipes and lines askew – then

arrive in steady blackness.
I listen from the flight deck
to the music of the spheres, glide
past the moon, the milky way,
finally disappear.

KNIFE THROWER

Warning 1

Suppose your desire is really your disgust,
your car-crash attraction the stuff of pain addiction?
Suppose each time the One walks into the room

you see a sort of halo crackle
a heat wave shimmy: desire/ disgust.
But the punch in your guts is a weakness

in the knees and you go across the room
and you hand him a flyer.
You hand him a flyer.

His reaction is in excess of the action, this
intrigues you. You want to calm him down,
so you explain and point to a friend,

She said she met you at a party,
she thought you'd be into this. The One
pauses to reassess ... fingers the flyer.

You're not hooked yet – you still think
he's weird: that halo, the awkwardness,
a kind of twitchiness – but you're starting

to ignore the signs, you're not listening
to your sixth sense.
Fair enough, first impressions might be wrong,

but sometimes, just sometimes, that first reaction
– the lick of fear, the recognition of another's
defensive-aggressive anxiety, could be spot on.

But this stance, this anger, charms you now
because you don't deserve it. So, even though
this man has no obvious beauty here is the thing:

you forget him, but when you meet again
something is there. What was repelling
has become compelling: the reckless air,

the halo space patches in to some reaction
of your own, some junky love affair
with highs and lows – your fear of losing.

    Suppose your desire was really your disgust,
    your car-crash attraction the stuff of pain addiction.
    Suppose each time the One walks into a room –

at that moment there is no affection,
no attraction, just a kind of curiosity,
and you hand him a flyer.

You let yourself be drawn
believing the cards are all in your hands.
You don't think it will matter much,

an affair.
You think the unlikeliness of it all
(the disgust?) will counter your desire,

and so you drop your guard, you play,
and you stay, and you let him in.
You handed him a flyer.

In black and white

She likes the way her skirt swirls, its stiffness.
She likes the way her shoe-heels clack
the pavement to attention. Their shine.
The way her stockings glimmer, and how
her jacket cuff has three velvet buttons,
neat in a line. She likes the way
her lashes curl and lengthen,
how her push up bra pushes up. Her silver
clutch bag clutches nicely. She smiles.

But if she was in colour she would not be this.
She would be cracked wood:
dense, dark, full of tiny knots.

Warning 2

Suppose your desire was really
your disgust, your car-crash attraction
a heat wave shimmy, a punch in the guts –
so you go across the room and you let him
in. You let him, let him in.

Why do you pick these people?

You once said, in a moment of lucidity, *Is it me?*
And your friend said, *Hey, you can't help*
the people you bump into. But you know
this isn't true, because yes, it was a coincidence
that both of you were there in that place,

but then you made a choice: you gave him a flyer,
and he *knew* where you'd be two weeks from now,
and he came and found you. Waited, drifted –
careful to ignore you at first – then slowly
homing in.

Reckless Sleeper

A man has lost his hat. In sleep he finds
an apple that reminds him of a red bow
that his sister used to wear in her hair.
Then he sees his mother holding out her hand,
but as he goes to take it
she becomes a mirror, and
a bird flies past the window as
curtains are drawn and candles lit.

It must be night,
or someone has died.
He can't see much.
His bed, over there,
has been made already.
He closes his eyes.

Warning 3

Though perhaps it wasn't quite like this, and maybe
you handed out plenty of flyers to plenty of people,
and the One was just one who came along by chance,

not because of you in particular, but just in a random way.
And maybe he'd have picked up a flyer from a bar anyway?
One you'd have left in a pile on a window ledge,

so you'd have met regardless, but with no homing in,
no plan, just a random search on a Saturday night:
chat-ups and try-outs till somebody stuck. You.

No destiny involved. Nothing sinister. You did *not*
invite it. Except that you look back and recall his walking
into a room. And you wonder at your first reaction,

that first impression you ignored.

Iain Stansfield would've been good for me

On my birthday we had a party and I
asked Iain to come. But somewhere after
midnight, being drunk and a bit lively,
I ran off with three friends to the Buzz,
a nightclub where they'd let us in for free.
We only stayed for half an hour to have
a dance, got back to find Iain had been – and gone.

Another time, another house, I shared
a bed with him. We kissed. He didn't
try it on, waiting for me to make
the next move. I gave off mixed signals…
By then there'd been some weirdness going on
with me and David (a man I shared the rent with)
so, maybe, I've remembered all this wrong?

A year later, after Iain had left town,
I wrote to him through our alumni association.
How sad is that?
By then, I'd had enough of cow-eyed boys
who drank too much. I'd realised that, even
if I hadn't been much good for him,
Iain Stansfield would've been good for me.

Parmesan

The first time I encountered Parmesan, I threw it out.
We were living in a tiny terraced house, spread
over three floors; two rooms per floor, except
the floor with the bathroom on. Four of us

plus Paddy's kids (on Tuesdays and weekends),
and the three dogs and two kittens, Derek and Mavis
– except one died and I can't remember which.
Mostly we lived in the kitchen, there was no

central heating so we'd have the cooker on
to keep warm. If they messed about, the dogs
were made to hang out in the roofed yard out back
(the house was that narrow, corrugated plastic

hemmed one wall to the next).
Paddy played piano in the kitchen.
The kitchen was the biggest room after
the top bedroom, so that's where the piano stood.

Besides, there wasn't room for all of us
in the front room, unless the kids doubled up
on laps and beanbags, which made a squeeze of it,
a Mexican wave when someone wanted in or out,

and always putting someone too close to the fire.
That summer we didn't use the front room much,
because of the business of hiding
from the Poll Tax man. And that time a brick

came through the window – a previous tenant
angry at Paddy, nearly decking me –
that put us off too. No surprise then,
we preferred to sit in the back kitchen.

To get back to the parmesan. I'd been
looking for a snack and thought the lump
of rindish yellow wrapped in clingfilm
was cheddar cheese gone stale ... When

Paddy found his treat was gone he wasn't
best pleased. I didn't understand what was up,
Parmesan? The powdered stuff in tubs?
When I understood what I had done I nearly

said I'd eaten it, not wanting to look
stupid. But in the end I did confess
to ignorance not greed: I'd fed his precious
lump to the dogs. Of course,

I offered to buy him some more, but Paddy said
it was all right. *Never mind.* For maybe a week
I felt a prat. Like when your friends are going on
about a band you've never heard of,

and you fake a knowing interest,
then die a thousand deaths when their single
comes on the radio and you go,
who's that?

Electra Complex

I nearly went out with a man called Iain,
same name as my Dad except with an extra ‘i’.
I now go out with someone
with the same surname as me,
Nichols, except with an extra ‘l’.
Same name as my Dad, Mr – .

You’re right, it was a bit odd at first.
Such a coincidence, but we got used to it.
And now I’m thinking (fingers crossed)
second time lucky.

Silent type

I would consider a deep sigh,
a steady look, even a
specific grunt in my direction.
What I do not want to consider

is your wry deflection, your
answer to my question:
'Do you not have anything to say to me?'
'... Is the kettle on?'

Your compliments include: *Your hair*
has grown long. I know
the Laws of Love and so do you.
Law IV states: the silent one in love is often king.

Written in ice

I still write poems about you,
I no longer show them to you.

I also write poems about geese
swimming underwater.

I have four poems about seals,
often they do not live for long.

I do not show these poems either.

The further adventures of Electra

Ones apon a time their lived a prinses Her mother was horrid to HER. One day a little boy came to Her House. He said to Her. Wiy are you sad. The prinses toued* Him. No one new wat to do. So they made a plan. One boy said we cod tae* Her away. NO said anuthe boy. The prinses said we will make a satchel* of me. Thenn we will put it in here. Then you will dres uq in different clothes.
Then She will not now how* you are.

[*here the page is turned over*]

So They did. They kiLLed her mother and got maRRIED. They had a special Wedding. At chanhc* On Sunday monning. It was very niee inded.

The End.

* toued = told
cod tae = could take
satchel = statue
now how = know who
chanhc = church

Notes:

1. We believe the child to have been six years of age at the time of writing this document.

2. Whilst the act of matricide complies with the Electra Complex, the lack of mention of the father is tricky … However, the boy who pleads for exile of the queen instead of her death, may be the father in textual disguise.

4. Murder not marriage is the true motivational drive. Marriage may be the writer's attempt to cover her tracks with a normal story convention.

5. Poor spelling can be accounted for by the age of the writer, however, is there significance to the substitution of 'satchel' for 'statue'?

NB. Dressing up/ disguise (and indeed cross-dressing) have continued to be a theme in the life of the writer as an adult.

Dr Roger Bedford

[With thanks to Mrs E Nichols for preservation of the original document, and her willingness to disclose it to the relevant authorities.]

Shift

In a strange house I shift in darkness two blankets deep
and then I see you, and you say something indistinct
about work, and there is a struggle in your voice.
Something distracts me and when I turn back
you are bleeding, and you say, *did you not see before?*

and all at once I know you have done this to yourself,
like a fist in the mouth   collision with a blunt object.
I see a stain at your neck, darker than
your bloody, screwed-up mouth, the mumbled words,
the dangling teeth, your screwed-up voice…

I notice that the neck does not concern me so much,
which is strange; it is your precious, precious mouth
that poleaxes me. The wound of your mouth.
And I am embracing you   appalled that I missed this
and fearful for us.

Corona

We are far apart,
in towns whose rivers mouth
different coastlines:
Liverpool and Teignmouth.
In olden times
we'd be lovers who'd
look up to the sky at
a pre-arranged time,
to the same stars, the same moon,
and think of the other, looking.
This evening though,
at half-past seven,
I switch on Coronation Street
and think of you, doing the same.

Rapunzel

When the sun shines her hair comes out
in clumps and when you look again
she is gone. She ties her laces
to the bus stop, and walks home barefoot.
Until the clouds return she will stay
in the garden shed, signal her needs to
the back living-room with her hands,
and later, when it gets dark, with a torch.
She drinks only cold tea, eats tins of prunes,
which you will take to her on a purple tray.
It's all over fairly soon, by the time
I wake from a dream of catfish
she is sitting at the table
her hair grown long again.

Notes

Bambi Woods – was the name of a 1970s porn star who disappeared after making just one film, *Debbie Does Dallas*.

Away from here – loosely based on a documentary made by Louis Theroux at a Nevada brothel.

A tea party – from an interview given by the son of Martin Bormann (Hitler's private secretary) to *The Sunday Times* in 2004.

The weakest point – Sir Christopher Wren had four children, not just the one son I mention.

Electra Complex – the opposite of the Oedipus Complex i.e. the daughter is supposed to be in love with her father.

Second Chance – Anne Green was executed for killing her baby in 1650. She was thought dead after her hanging but revived later on the dissection table.

Second Sight – Ursula Shipton was born illegitimately in a cave in 1488. She later became known for her ability to prophesise and her political wile.

At the haberdashery counter, My name – In 2006 I met a woman whose aunt, Meirion Evans, had lost an eye when the Lusitania was bombed.

Frank Woolworth founded his empire in the USA. His brother ran the UK franchise, whose flagship store opened in 1909 in Liverpool. http://museum.woolworths.co.uk

Rapunzel – the starting point for the shape of this poem was Charles Bennett's 'Only her lips remember'.